W9-CHK-885

Science-Hobby Book of
Weather Forecasting

Study these symbols to help you interpret your daily newspaper weather m

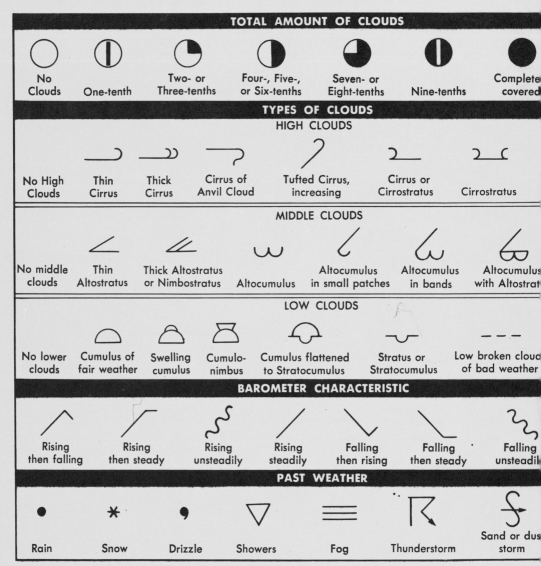

TOTAL AMOUNT OF CLOUDS

| No Clouds | One-tenth | Two- or Three-tenths | Four-, Five-, or Six-tenths | Seven- or Eight-tenths | Nine-tenths | Completely covered |

TYPES OF CLOUDS

HIGH CLOUDS

| No High Clouds | Thin Cirrus | Thick Cirrus | Cirrus of Anvil Cloud | Tufted Cirrus, increasing | Cirrus or Cirrostratus | Cirrostratus |

MIDDLE CLOUDS

| No middle clouds | Thin Altostratus | Thick Altostratus or Nimbostratus | Altocumulus | Altocumulus in small patches | Altocumulus in bands | Altocumulus with Altostrat |

LOW CLOUDS

| No lower clouds | Cumulus of fair weather | Swelling cumulus | Cumulo-nimbus | Cumulus flattened to Stratocumulus | Stratus or Stratocumulus | Low broken cloud of bad weather |

BAROMETER CHARACTERISTIC

| Rising then falling | Rising then steady | Rising unsteadily | Rising steadily | Falling then rising | Falling then steady | Falling unsteadil |

PAST WEATHER

| Rain | Snow | Drizzle | Showers | Fog | Thunderstorm | Sand or dus storm |

Sky
obscured

rocumulus
d Cirrus

Altocumulus
in tufts

Arrow
n any cloud
mbol shows
direction
of motion

Falling
steadily

Cloudy or
overcast

Science-Hobby Book of
Weather Forecasting

by
ROBERT WELLS

Published by
LERNER PUBLICATIONS COMPANY
Minneapolis, Minnesota

to
Christopher

Second Printing 1971

Revised edition copyright © 1968 by Lerner Publications Company
Original copyright © MCMLXII by Hammond Incorporated

International Standard Book Number: 0-8225-0559-2
Library of Congress Catalog Card Number: 68-54183

CONTENTS

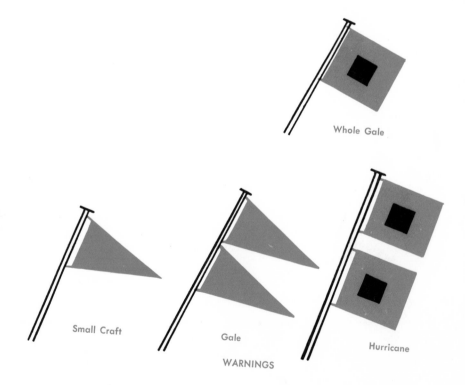

Whole Gale

Small Craft

Gale

WARNINGS

Hurricane

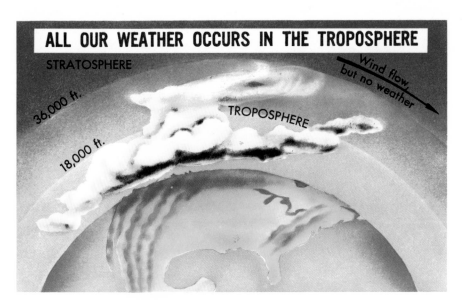

ALL OUR WEATHER OCCURS IN THE TROPOSPHERE

STRATOSPHERE

Wind flow, but no weather

36,000 ft.

18,000 ft.

TROPOSPHERE

Weather Forecasting as a Hobby

WEATHER-EYE FORECASTING

"What will the weather be?"

Come outdoors and look up. Is the sky covered with big, black, low-hanging clouds? What is your forecast? "Rain likely," you say promptly — and you probably are right.

Or, when you look up, is the sky sparkling clear, with only an occasional fluffy white cloud sailing across it, high and fast? What now is your weather prediction? "That's easy," you answer, "fair." Again you probably are right.

At this point you are already, as you can see, something of a weather forecaster. Certainly your procedure has been much the same as the professional meteorologist's. You observed the conditions — in this case, of the sky — and then you matched these against your knowledge of how weather behaves. Since rain comes from clouds, you predicted "no rain" when you saw almost no clouds, or "rain likely" when you saw clouds of the type you know usually bring rain.

Of course, the professional meteorologist has more knowledge of what makes weather behave as it does. He has a variety of instruments — probably including an electronic computer — to help him. With these, he can predict more accurately, farther ahead, and for a wider area, than can the amateur who is not as well equipped.

As an amateur, you have the choice to make your hobby as small or large as you wish. You may be perfectly satisfied to predict, from the clouds above you, what your own local weather probably will be within the next few hours. However doing "only" that, *accurately*, is not quite as easy as it sounds, for weather has a habit of changing unexpectedly.

Navy aircraft over eye of
"Hurricane Gracie"

U.S. Navy photo

You may find that you want to purchase or construct instruments of your own and to learn to read and predict from weather maps which appear daily in newspapers. Your predictions then may be more accurate for a day or even two days ahead. Some amateurs, using these techniques, enjoy predicting the weather for distant parts of the country. They keep score of how well — or poorly — they did.

This book is intended to provide information to satisfy both types of hobbyists. It won't make a good weatherman of you; that is something you must do for yourself. But it will show you how to go about weather forecasting, and it will provide you with enough information to start your hobby. Then when you are ready for more detailed, scientific information, you will refer to it.

Whether hobbyist or professional, the more carefully and accurately you observe, the more accurate will be your forecast. Accurate, too, should be your records of these observations and of the weather that follows them, if such records are to help you forecast accurately. These records will tell you what to expect of the weather when next you observe conditions such as the ones you have observed and recorded. For even though weather is subject to surprise changes, it does follow a cause-and-effect pattern. Therefore, the more you can see of the pattern, the more accurately you should be able to decide what weather will follow "these" conditions, here, and now.

Causes of weather are described more completely farther on in the book. Their action takes place in the air. These causes are affected by the surface of our rotating earth and are energized by the rays from our sun some ninety-three million miles away. Complex and distant though all this may appear, the clouds over your head can tell you a great deal about what weather to expect here, soon. So, come outdoors again and look up.

FORECASTING BY CLOUDS

You will see, now that you are observing more closely, that clouds come in a variety of shapes and sizes. Also, you will find some float quite high in the sky; others, quite low; still others, at levels between those two. Since the shapes of these clouds are different and their altitudes are different, they must have been formed in different ways. Certainly, then, the weather effects they will produce will also differ. It is quite possible to weather forecast, locally and for several hours ahead, by these clouds. The following are the most common and most easily identified:

The fluffy white cloud you see most frequently sailing serenely across the blue summer sky is the *cumulus*. Its dome-shaped top and rounded edges are often much lighter colored than the body of the cloud which darkens when it moves directly overhead, or lightens when it once more reflects the sun. The underside — the base — of this cloud is quite level and usually only some 1,500 to 6,000 feet high. This is low for clouds; however, this cloud's base sometimes rides as high as 10,000 feet. Cumulus is a fair-weather cloud — providing it remains separate and does not show signs of building.

You may observe this cloud growing in height — developing vertically — as the day wears on from morning when it is first formed. Sometimes this cloud "boils up" to a height of five miles or more. Then the cloud is a different type, even though remaining something of the same cumulus family. It is now a *cumulo-nimbus*, a rain cloud. This towering, steep-sided monster is a familiar sight, as it rolls up to and then over you, a storm complete with flashes of lightning and rolls of thunder accompanied by strong gusts of wind that send leaves and dust swirling high into the darkness close above. Then comes the rain.

A truly low-altitude cloud — usually no higher than one mile — is the *stratocumulus*. Again, this is a round-appearing cloud. But instead of being separate from others, this cloud forms in a layer — a stratus — of billows of cumulus. Very often this layer is solid, or almost so. Still soft looking and rounded, as cumulus is, the stratocumulus now has lost the brightness of the separate fair-weather cumulus cloud. Gray, dark in places, these rolls of clouds join together with only a few open spots, if any. The base has more of a wavy look than the flatter base of the cumulus. When they blanket the sky they appear to promise rain, yet this type of cloud does not usually produce precipitation. If there is any rain or snow at all, it is light. This is the cloud whose proper name includes the title "vesperalis" to connote that it is an "evening" cloud. And it is that, generally — but not always.

Still higher up there may also be another group of clouds. Again, these are of the cumulus type: high cumulus — or, by its proper name, *altocumulus*. It keeps certain of the cumulus-family features, too. But now that it is at a level of lighter, more rarified atmosphere, this cloud is lighter, smaller, less dense in itself and in its grouping with similar ones. Still, it is the rounded cumulus — although flattened a bit, now, on top. And, like the vesperalis, it may be seen toward evening, but more often at night. When it floats between you and the moon or the sun, if it should appear during the day, that

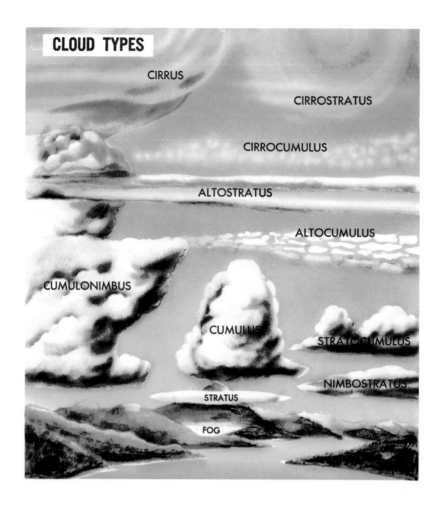

CLOUD TYPES

CIRRUS

CIRROSTRATUS

CIRROCUMULUS

ALTOSTRATUS

ALTOCUMULUS

CUMULONIMBUS

CUMULUS

STRATOCUMULUS

NIMBOSTRATUS

STRATUS

FOG

body will have small colored rings around it: blue, inside the circles; red, outside, called a corona.

Masses of little altocumulus often appear in layers, and sometimes these various levels crisscross in different directions. In themselves, altocumulus clouds are not necessarily rain clouds, but they can serve as an alert to an approaching storm if you notice that any rings around moon or sun are growing smaller.

Imagine a display of altocumulus — still higher, and still more fleecy, spread out over a still wider area. Here, at 30,000-foot heights — or even higher — is the *cirrocumulus*. Still puffs of clouds and thereby keeping the "cumulus" designation, these now are in the high-altitude group of cirrus clouds. It is much colder up here so the cirrocumulus clouds are composed not of water droplets but of ice crystals. These groups of small flakes of clouds — lines of them — are so high and thin that they resemble the scales of fish. This is the "mackerel" sky so popular in weather folk-sayings as a messenger of changing weather. When you observe cirrocumulus, you also will see others of the cirrus high-altitude family of clouds.

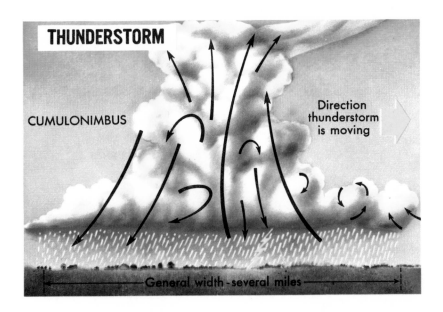

One may be formed from the very top of a cumulonimbus (as high sometimes as 40,000 feet), blowing free from the cloud's main body. That part is the distinctive "anvil" — the ice-crystal head of the cumulonimbus. It points forward in the direction that the winds are moving the storm which the great cloud below is bringing. Then the anvil-shaped cloud is known as the thunder cirrus. There are two other forms of cirrus; one often in the shape of a long comma, the other in the shape of filaments — either straight or bent. These clouds are silky looking, although their edges appear ragged. They look delicate and fibrous.

Different from the low-flying cumulus which seems to float by so rapidly, the cirrus at its great height seems to move hardly at all. The winds at that altitude, however, may be pushing it at nearly two miles a minute. Height also makes it possible for this cloud — usually white — to take on color when the sun appears to be below the horizon. When this happens, you will see this cloud illumined with the refractions of the yellow-orange-red end of the color spectrum. These are the "mare's tails" which — if they are dominant in the sky — usually promise continued fair weather.

Cirrostratus, as its name tells you, is a sheet of these thin veil-like clouds. Sometimes it is so diffuse that the sky just looks milky. Often it almost fills the sky and is so thin, usually, that the sun shines right through it, and you can observe shadows on the ground. You also will notice, then, a large halo around the sun — or moon. But now the coloring is reversed from the rings of the altocumulus. Here the blue is outside the ring. This is a cloud which frequently means not only change in weather, but a change to bad weather.

When a layered, stratus cloud is observed below the great heights of the cirrus, and is at the medium height for clouds — 6,000 to 20,000 feet — it is recognized as *altostratus*. Altostratus appears fibrous and is usually thicker at this lower level of heavier atmosphere. Often it is thick enough to obscure even the sun; yet often it is so thin that even the moon can shine through. But the composition of this bluish-gray cloud is such that, when the sun does shine through, its rays cast no shadow — an additional identifying feature of altostratus.

Lower — at about the same height as stratocumulus — is the *nimbostratus:* layered rain cloud. It is thicker than the altostratus from which it may have developed by thickening downward. Ice crystals usually are at its upper surface. A distinguishing feature is the strange, dim lighting which seems to come from within this dark, gray cloud. Its base looks ragged, and you can almost feel the rain coming when you look at it. Rain may be falling, in fact, but not necessarily reaching the ground. When rain does reach the ground from this cloud, it usually persists longer than does rain from other cloud types.

Still lower, now fairly close to the ground, is the *stratus.* This indefinitely shaped, drizzly looking cloud is the one you often see around a hilltop. Unlike the persistent rains and snows from its higher relative, the nimbostratus, only drizzle or light snow — if that much — comes from stratus. "Scud" cloud refers to stratus which the wind has shredded, or broken — *fractostratus* is its proper name. These shreds are wind-driven at so low a height that they appear to race along. This speed generally is an illusion, created by relative height. If, instead of breaking up, this stratus descends until it reaches the ground, you know it as fog.

FORECASTING BY WINDS AND CLOUDS

So, here you are, back on the ground again — or, at least, not looking up so high. You are probably wondering *why* there are so many types of clouds and *what* makes them into these different shapes?

Part of the answer to your question is the air itself — in movement. When air moves vertically, this movement is called an air current. When air moves horizontally, it is known as wind. The wind not only has something to do with cloud shapes; it also brings the clouds overhead and then moves them on.

It is not just the clouds, alone, which will tell you what the weather is going to be. It is also the wind in conjunction with the clouds — what it does to bring them, to change them, to move them away— that gives you the signs of what weather probably will soon be here. So, look up again. See how the clouds you have come to recognize in their different shapes and at their different altitudes now *change.* See how they move, at what speeds, and in which directions. It is these changes, directions, and speeds (more than the *present* shapes of the clouds) which tell you what the weather probably is going to be.

Here are some guides.

Cumulus, not growing until afternoon:
Fair weather, winds holding, sky clear by night

Cumulus growing before noon, building high during the afternoon and increasing; humid:
Showers before evening. Freshening winds from SW

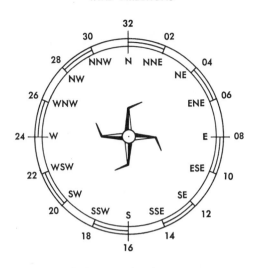

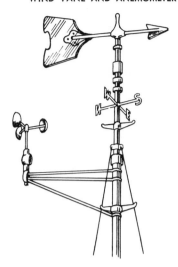

Cumulonimbus moving in separate masses from the S or SW:
> Thundershowers, with lightning and hail possible, strong gusts in the afternoon or evening. Fresh winds from the direction the clouds have come

Cumulonimbus banked in line from the N, NW, or W, while strong surface winds come out of the S or SW:
> Squalls imminent, to be followed by big thunderstorms. Wind shifting, to come out of the NW or W, followed by clearing and cooler

Stratocumulus banked in line from the N or NW, while strong surface winds come out of the S, SW, or W:
> Squalls; short bursts of rain, followed by clearing and cooler

Stratocumulus in rolls, remaining round looking; breaks showing open sky; clouds moving in surface wind's direction:
> Little change expected for the next twenty-four hours

Stratocumulus join together, grow darker and duller; generally overcast the sky:
> Occasional rain

Stratocumulus overcast breaks increasingly into separate masses which rise; winds hold out of the W:
> Clearing and cooler

Altocumulus, in groups, moving fast out of the NW or W, while surface winds grow stronger out of the SW or S:
> Squalls possible. Surface wind may shift and match upper air wind. Brief but heavy rain, followed by clearing and cooler

Altocumulus come from the S or SW and join together into layers; if there is a corona (ring around sun or moon) and it gradually grows smaller; surface winds E:
> Precipitation likely between six and twelve hours, followed by SE winds changing to SW. Partly cloudy and warmer

13

Altocumulus in separate masses or long patches, moving in same direction as that of surface wind; sky visible through breaks:
    Continued fair

Cirrus, cirrostratus, cirrocumulus remaining white and in wispy patches:
    Continued fair

Cirrus, cirrostratus, cirrocumulus darkening, lowering, thickening; moving out of the S or SW, while surface winds come out of the E:
    Precipitation likely within a day. Winds from E or SE, changing to SW and freshening. Warmer

FORECASTING BY WINDS AND BAROMETER

It is easy to perceive the important part wind plays in weather-making. But from where does the wind get its force? What makes the wind blow, moving the rain and snow clouds overhead, and then moving them on, leaving the sky clear for warm sunlight?

The answer begins some ninety-three million miles away — at the sun. The heat which results from the sun's rays warms the air. The air rises, as does a balloon filled with warm air. Not all areas of the air are warmed equally. Some receive more heat, largely because they happen to be over an area of earth's surface which reflects the sun's rays more strongly. Fly in a light airplane on a sunny summer day, over a field green with vegetation and then over a field newly plowed and bare. When your small airplane starts over the ploughed field, it will lift almost as if it were in an elevator. The warmed air, rising more strongly and faster, from the better-reflecting bare earth, has force enough to lift your airplane with it. Other air must come to replace this rising air: there can be no such thing as a hole in the air — an "air pocket." Other air does come — from areas where the air is not being heated as much. It comes, moving in a general horizontal plane, from another area to this. As you know, air moving horizontally is identified as wind. (Rising columns of air are air currents. If there were considerable moisture in

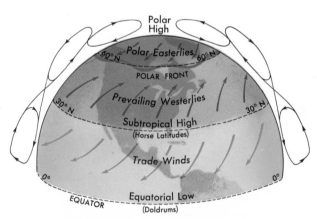

GENERAL CIRCULATION OF
THE ATMOSPHERE

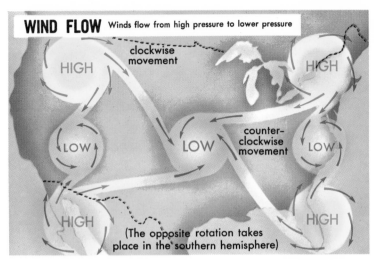

WIND FLOW Winds flow from high pressure to lower pressure

clockwise movement

HIGH

HIGH

counter-clockwise movement

LOW

LOW

LOW

HIGH

HIGH

(The opposite rotation takes place in the southern hemisphere)

that air, the rising currents might "boil up" a cumulus until it becomes a towering miles-high cumulonimbus.)

Since you will want to know not only wind direction but also wind speed, the following is a guide for estimating wind speeds. It is associated with the sailor's guide worked out last century by a British Admiral, Sir Francis Beaufort:

Name of wind	Speed, mph	Specifications
Calm	less than 1	Smoke rises straight up. Trees are still, water is mirror calm.
Light air	1-3	Smoke drifts in direction of wind. Leaves on trees move slightly.
Light breeze	4-7	Wind can be felt on face. Leaves rustle. Wind vanes respond.
Gentle breeze	8-12	Leaves in constant motion. Light flags flap.
Moderate breeze	13-18	Small branches move, dust and other light debris are stirred up.
Fresh breeze	19-24	Young leafy trees sway. Dust stirred up in clouds. Crested wavelets on lakes, ponds.
Strong breeze	25-31	Tree boughs swing. Wind whistles through telephone wires.
Moderate gale	32-38	Tree trunks swing. Difficult walking against the wind.
Fresh gale	39-46	Walking requires effort. Small branches break loose.
Strong gale	47-54	Slight damage to buildings, overhead signs, large windows.
Whole gale	55-63	Trees blown down. Considerable damage to buildings. (More often experienced, however, at sea.)
Storm	64-74	(Rare.) Wide damage.
Hurricane	75 or more	Great damage, wide destruction.

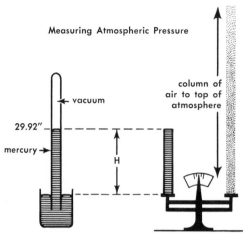

Measuring Atmospheric Pressure

vacuum

column of
air to top of
atmosphere

29.92″

mercury

H

H.=Height of mercury column that is balanced by corresponding column of air. (Standard atmospheric pressure at sea level=29.92″ of mercury)

These winds of varying forces, move to fill — with cooler air — what otherwise would be that highly improbable "hole in the air" due to air rising because it was warmed. But what *moves* the cooler air — or, to say it another way, what furnishes the force which makes winds "blow"?

The answer is pressure — atmospheric pressure. It is another important factor in the making of weather, and in predicting it. This is how it works:

The air, our atmosphere, is not a "nothingness." It has mass. Since it also closely surrounds our earth — indeed is a part of our world — it is subjected to the pull of earth's gravity. This is another way of saying that *air* has weight. Because air has weight, air can exert pressure. At sea level — the lowest level of our atmosphere and, therefore, at the bottom of all the weight of all the air lying above — the average pressure of air is about 14.7 pounds per square inch. Nor is this pressure exerted only in a "down" direction; it is also exerted on all sides and upward. This pressure provides the force that can move air from one place, where pressure is higher, to another place where it is lower.

As winds blow, they may bring with them warmth or cold, moisture or dryness. If you can discover whether your area is in a high-pressure or a low-pressure zone at a given time, you can anticipate what kind of weather changes may soon come. You can do that more accurately if, together with information about pressure, you also know from which area the wind is coming, for example, from a warm dry area or a cold wet area.

Learn these two sets of information. Wind direction can be felt; or seen by its effects on weather vanes, dust, or leaves; or observed in the directions of cloud movement. Atmospheric pressure can be measured by the barometer. The readings are on the face of the dial of the aneroid type, or on the scale of the mercurial type which resembles a thermometer. They are calibrated in inches and hundredths, the usual range being 29.80 to 30.20 inches. To say that the barometer is falling, means that it is registering a lower number than it registered a little while ago. This means that the weight of the atmosphere is growing lighter.

16

Here are some U.S. Weather Bureau guides for using barometric pressure and wind direction information:

Wind direction	Sea-level barometric pressure (inches)	Weather indicated
SW to NW	30.10 to 30.20, steady	Fair with little temperature change for 1 to 2 days
SW to NW	30.10 to 30.20, rising rapidly	Fair followed within 2 days by rain; warmer
SW to NW	30.20 and above, steady	Continued fair, no marked temperature change
SW to NW	30.20 and above, falling slowly	Fair with slightly rising temperature for 2 days
S to SE	30.10 to 30.20, falling slowly	Rain within 24 hours
S to SE	30.10 to 30.20, falling rapidly	Wind increasing, rain within 12 to 24 hours
SE to NE	30.10 to 30.20, falling slowly	Rain in 12 to 18 hours
SE to NE	30.10 to 30.20, falling rapidly	Increasing wind, rain within 12 hours hours
E to NE	30.10 to 30.20, falling slowly	(Winter) Rain within 24 hours (Summer) With light winds, rain may not occur for several days
E to NE	30.10 and above, falling rapidly	(Winter) Rain or snow, with increasing winds (Summer) Rain probably within 12 to 24 hours
SE to NE	30.00 or below, falling slowly	Rain will continue 1 to 2 days
SE to NE	30.00 or below, falling rapidly	Rain with high winds, followed in 36 hours by clearing, cooler
S to SW	30.00 or below, rising slowly	Clearing within a few hours, fair for several days
S to E	29.80 or below, falling rapidly	Severe storm soon, followed within 24 hours by clearing and, in winter, colder
E to N	29.80 or below, falling rapidly	Severe NE gale and heavy precipitation (Winter) Heavy snow, followed by cold wave
Going to W	29.80 or below, rising rapidly	Clearing and colder

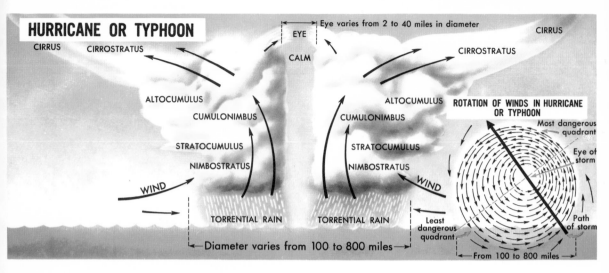

These guides are general; your own part of the country may experience some differences. But you can see how desirable it is to keep records of *your* weather in order to modify such guides for forecasting within your own area. Another guide is given below.

Generally, if the barometer falls steadily, and

1 — The wind comes from an easterly quarter, expect foul weather; clearing and fair weather will follow after the wind shifts to come out of a westerly quarter.

2 — The wind comes from the S or SE, expect a storm from the W or NW; the center will pass near or to the north, between 12 and 24 hours hence. Wind will shift to S, then SW to NW.

3 — The wind comes from the E or NE, expect a storm from the S or SW; its center will pass near or to the south, between 12 and 24 hours hence. Wind will shift to N, then NW.

(Note: The faster and farther the barometer falls, the earlier and stronger will be the storm.)

What you should have for weather forecasting is not so much a single reading as the *trend* in the course of a series of readings. You look to see if there is a change (a rise or a fall), *how much* of a change, and the *rate* of that change. You are interested less in what *is* the weather, than in what *will* the weather *be*. Look for signs in the trend of what you are observing: what is happening to the barometric pressure, the wind direction and velocity, and the temperature — it usually rises just before a storm. Observe the shape, height, appearance, amount, and direction of movement of the clouds, and the changes in these.

Don't regard each piece of information as a separate or isolated event but, rather, as a part to be fitted and used together to produce a forecast. It would be a careless detective indeed who would use only one clue instead of the many available to him — or who would not see the relationship between clues which would yield him the pattern of what he is seeking.

FORECASTING BY WEATHER PROVERBS

If you observe, recognize, and use weather signs of your own locale, you will find good use for weather proverbs, too. These should be adapted to what you observe of weather elements in your own locale, as with the table of barometric pressure and winds. Such tables and proverbs are only generalizations. Fortunately, you are not in the position of your ancestors who had no weather instruments except their own senses to help them. For them — farmers, sailors, shepherds, fishermen — weather forecasting was no hobby. The livelihood and well-being of their families were endangered when the weather ruined their crops, sank their ships, froze or parched their livestock. No wonder they observed the weather so closely and devised weather sayings which father carefully taught son. Here are some which you may find useful *if* they apply to *your* area.

Rainbow to windward, foul fall the day; rainbow to landward,
rain runs away.
Thunder in the morning, rain before night.
Who soweth in rain shall reap with tears.
The north wind doth blow, and we shall have snow.
If wind follows sun, fair weather will come.
If clouds fight the wind, a storm will begin.
Rain before seven, lift before eleven.
How thy garments are warm, when He quieteth the Earth by the
South wind. (Job)
Mackerel scales, furl your sails.
Fog from seaward, fair weather; fog from landward, rain. (Typical
New England!)
The farther the sight, the nearer the rain.
When sounds are clear, rain is near.
(Wind from) Northwest is far the best; northeast is bad for man
and beast.

Moisture, temperature, barometric pressure and other elements, which make up weather, have their effects upon animals and insects as well as upon plants, all of which display weather signs if you can identify them. When atmospheric pressure drops, our own internal body pressure may, by contrast, feel greater and so produce headache or toothache. Probably this happens to animals, too, and may account for their restless behavior just before a storm. When air is moisture-laden, wings of insects become wet and heavy, causing the insect to fly lower than usual. You may not see these insects as easily as you do the birds darting to feed on them as they fly. It is easy to understand the saying, "When insects fly low, rain comes yet not slow."

Can you explain the following?
Early insects, early spring, good crops. (Apache)
If pigeons (or other birds) return slowly to the nest, it will rain.
Houseflies coming into the house mean rain.
Flies on the ceiling mean rain.
Smoke bending to the ground means rain.

Sensitive plants contract their leaves when rain is coming.

Pimpernel, Pimpernel tell me true; whether the weather be fine or no?

If animals crowd together, rain will follow.

Horses sweating in the stable is a sign of rain.

When a cow tries to scratch her ear, it means a shower is very near;

when she thumps her ribs with tail, look for lightning, thunder, hail.

THE LOCAL FORECAST

There is no reason why you, after sufficient observation of local weather, can't devise your own weather proverbs.

With all these tables, signs, and sayings, you should be able to predict local weather with some degree of accuracy for a short period. Your accuracy of forecast will depend on a number of things, one of which is to adapt this information to your observation of weather. Frequent practice gives the forecaster intuition — that special sixth sense which no superefficient electronic computer has yet acquired.

U.S. Weather Bureau

Wires sagging from the weight of ice

If you want to combine some of the elements of weather information you have just acquired and use them for still more accurate forecasting, here are some guides:

Weather should remain fair if

the barometrical reading stays steady or rises.

the wind stays steady out of the west.

the sun is not obscured by clouds when it sets.

in summer, morning mists dissipate well before noon.

you see fewer puffy cumulus clouds in the afternoon than you saw
in the morning.

temperatures remain no higher than normal — and wind and sky
are as described above.

Weather should not remain fair if
>the barometrical reading falls — and continues to fall.
>the sun, when it sets, is covered by thin clouds or a mass of heavy moist-looking clouds.
>puffy cumulus clouds increase in number, grow dark, and descend.
>mare's tails (cirrus) increase in number and gradually level out into cirrostratus and a halo is observed around the moon or sun.
>clouds move by in more than one level and direction.
>temperature does not drop after sunset.

U.S. Weather Bureau

Results of storm damage

>you can barely see *any* stars.
>there is a ring around the moon or sun.
>the wind shifts from the west, or lessens.

Rainy weather may come
>in the afternoon, within an hour, when the cumulus clouds overhead build high, and the sky to the SW grows dark.
>within a few hours, if the thermometer's reading in the morning is high, the air feels humid, and *you* feel uncomfortable and if there are cumulus clouds.
>within a day, following the change of cirrus clouds into heavier cirrostratus, and you see a halo around the sun or moon.

Fair weather should follow if
>there is a rapid rise in reading of your barometer.
>the sun breaks through between clouds.
>an overcast sky opens into patches showing clear sky.
>clouds rise and their color grows lighter.
>the winds begin to blow mainly from the W or NW.
>it grows cooler.
>the sunset sky has a deep pink color.
>the sky clears.

Cooler weather should follow if

> the barometrical readings rise.
>
> the sun at setting shows clearly after a cloudy day.
>
> clouds appear to be firm — not loose and rainy-looking.
>
> the wind shifts to the N.
>
> a sunny day doesn't bring a rise in temperature.

Warmer weather should come if

> the barometrical readings show that a storm may be approaching.
>
> the setting sun is one great fireball.
>
> clouds cover the night sky.
>
> the wind changes direction from N or W to S usually, or E.

Again, a combination of indications — rather than isolated indications — will give you a better basis for making a more accurate forecast. Barometer, thermometer, weather vane, and close observation of changes in cloud structures and heights will combine to provide the best basis for your predictions, which will improve as you continue to gain experience. You will find often that the weather for your area frequently differs, however slightly, from that only a few miles away. Features of the terrain — hills, woods, fields, valleys; or man-made features of many factory smokestacks or masses of automobile exhausts — often affect local temperatures, cloudiness, or precipitation. The chill, moisture-laden winds blowing off the Pacific Ocean bring San Francisco fog and cool summers, but they are stopped by high mountains. Sacramento, on the other side, gets no wind and bakes comfortably in dry, hot sunshine. Where is *your* home? What are the characteristics of earth's surface there? Is your house in a valley into which, at night, cool air slides down from the slopes of the hills around you? Certainly you'll sleep with more blankets on your bed than will your neighbor on the hill.

What is the history of *your* weather? Records, easy enough to keep, will almost certainly improve your accuracy in forecasting. Even a weather station's records contain little more than these items, observed on schedule several times each day:

> The present weather
>
> Direction of wind and its speed (near the ground)
>
> Cloud formation, amount of clouds, their height
>
> Temperature of the air and its humidity
>
> Present barometric pressure and whether it seems to be rising, holding, or falling
>
> The changes that have occurred since the previous observation

The professional meteorologist uses this information to acquaint himself — in as much detail as possible — with what the weather now is. After that, he can apply his knowledge of the causes of these conditions. Coupling this information with information of the present weather, he prepares his forecast.

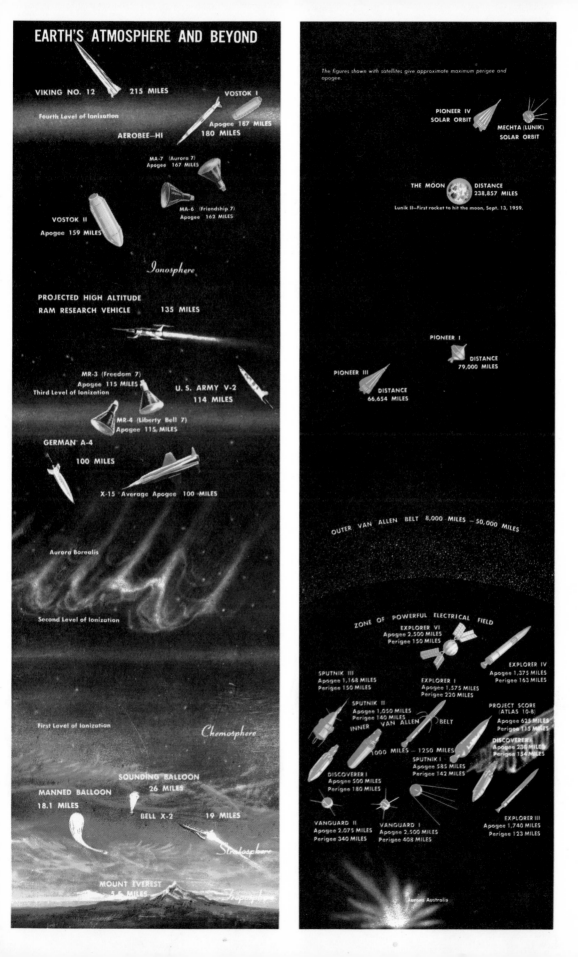

EARTH'S ATMOSPHERE AND BEYOND

VIKING NO. 12   215 MILES

Fourth Level of Ionization

VOSTOK I
Apogee 187 MILES

AEROBEE—HI   180 MILES

MA-7 (Aurora 7)
Apogee 167 MILES

MA-6 (Friendship 7)
Apogee 162 MILES

VOSTOK II
Apogee 159 MILES

Ionosphere

PROJECTED HIGH ALTITUDE
RAM RESEARCH VEHICLE   135 MILES

MR-3 (Freedom 7)
Apogee 115 MILES

Third Level of Ionization

U. S. ARMY V-2
114 MILES

MR-4 (Liberty Bell 7)
Apogee 115 MILES

GERMAN A-4
100 MILES

X-15 Average Apogee 100 MILES

Aurora Borealis

Second Level of Ionization

First Level of Ionization

Chemosphere

SOUNDING BALLOON
26 MILES

MANNED BALLOON
18.1 MILES

BELL X-2   19 MILES

Stratosphere

MOUNT EVEREST
5.5 MILES

Troposphere

The figures shown with satellites give approximate maximum perigee and apogee.

PIONEER IV
SOLAR ORBIT

MECHTA (LUNIK)
SOLAR ORBIT

THE MOON   DISTANCE
238,857 MILES

Lunik II—First rocket to hit the moon, Sept. 13, 1959.

PIONEER I
DISTANCE
79,000 MILES

PIONEER III
DISTANCE
66,654 MILES

OUTER VAN ALLEN BELT   8,000 MILES — 50,000 MILES

ZONE OF POWERFUL ELECTRICAL FIELD

EXPLORER VI
Apogee 2,500 MILES
Perigee 150 MILES

EXPLORER IV
Apogee 1,375 MILES
Perigee 163 MILES

SPUTNIK III
Apogee 1,168 MILES
Perigee 150 MILES

EXPLORER I
Apogee 1,575 MILES
Perigee 220 MILES

PROJECT SCORE
(ATLAS 10-B)
Apogee 625 MILES
Perigee 115 MILES

SPUTNIK II
Apogee 1,050 MILES
Perigee 140 MILES

INNER   VAN ALLEN   BELT

DISCOVERER
Apogee 236 MILES
Perigee 154 MILES

SPUTNIK I
Apogee 585 MILES
Perigee 142 MILES

1000 MILES — 1250 MILES

DISCOVERER I
Apogee 500 MILES
Perigee 180 MILES

VANGUARD II
Apogee 2,075 MILES
Perigee 340 MILES

VANGUARD I
Apogee 2,500 MILES
Perigee 408 MILES

EXPLORER III
Apogee 1,740 MILES
Perigee 123 MILES

Aurora Australis

SOME BASICS FOR SCIENTIFIC FORECASTING
WHY WEATHER CHANGES

Consider the composition of the atmosphere and its behavior. What an extraordinary substance must be this combination of gases! You cannot see it or smell it or taste it or feel it or hear it — or live without it. It is highly compressible and yet can expand so indefinitely that it is hard to say just how far out our atmosphere does, finally, disappear into the emptiness of space. It can gently bend a blade of grass or support the weight of a hurtling multi-ton airplane. It can be warm here and cool there; rising here, lowering there; light here, heavy there; moving in "this" direction here, in "that" direction there; sodden with water vapor here, dry there. It conducts lightning's powerful flashes as easily as it conducts the sound of a baby's cry. It conducts pulses of energy which come from the sun, admitting those which sustain life and filtering out those which would destroy it.

This is our atmosphere. The place where weather is made and continually changed is the troposphere (atmosphere's lowest level) only five miles high over the poles, eleven over the equator. So fluid is it, there is no wonder the weather it produces is variable. Here exists the possibility for an almost endless number of variations in weather, the reason weather forecasting is not an easy job. It would be on the moon. For each lunar day, you could forecast, "Fair and very hot" and, for each lunar night, "Fair and very cold." For, on the moon, there is scarcely any atmosphere.

The composition of our own atmosphere below some 30,000 feet is nitrogen (77%) which our plant life uses extensively; oxygen (20%) which we and other animals require; a few other, minor gases; and changing quantities of water vapor, coming principally from the oceans, which is necessary to all life. Water vapor plays such an important part in the making of our weather that some meteorologists think of our atmosphere chiefly as water

Port of New York Authority

A weather balloon being released at Weather Bureau installations, New York International Airport.

vapor, thinned out. This water vapor forms clouds which *tell* about the weather, often *are the weather* (rain or snow), and *return* moisture to refresh the soil.

The lifting of sufficient moisture in the atmosphere to make a huge thundercloud of rain requires energy. Energy also is required to run the machine called "weather." That energy comes from the sun, some ninety-three million miles away, at the speed of light. It is in the form of shortwave radiation, rather like radio waves or light waves. It is this energy, striking earth's surface, which sets the molecules dancing harder and produces heat.

This is also the heat which has so much to do with producing weather. As the earth rotates, our day which was heated by the sun's rays becomes night, now cool from the absence of those heat-producing rays. As the earth revolves about the sun in the course of our year, the sun's rays fall almost *directly* upon our area during one part of the year — summer. In winter, these rays *slant* upon our area; they are diffused and thus weaker. As a result, our winter months are colder.

There are still other factors which produce unevenness in heating of the earth's surface and, in turn, of the air resting on top of it. The ploughed field and the green field is one example: light colors reflect the sun's rays much better than do dark colors. The difference in heat-absorbing versus heat-reflecting qualities of land and water also accounts for unevenness in heating. Considering how much of earth's surface is water, this factor of contrast is a major one. Finally, the tilt of earth's axis changes the seasons in the different parts of the world, heating some now more, now less.

These factors are a few of the ways in which earth's surface — and therefore its atmosphere — becomes heated in one area and cooled in another. Air movement is an important contributor to the making of weather. Air in one area is heated; it rises, perhaps forms rain-giving clouds. Air in another area — not heated as much — moves, under pressure from the atmosphere, to the area being vacated and brings its own temperatures, water vapor content, and pressure. These may be changed, en route, by areas over which they travel.

Earth's rotation, every day, keeps this series of motion systems in a state of continuing change further altered by seasons. The atmosphere is incessantly in motion as is the entire universe. Were it not for the orderliness of these systems, there could be no predictability — and no basis for weather forecasting. But natural systems *are* orderly — even though the variations are more than enough to make forecasting an uncertain activity, at best.

Mountains also play a part in the unequal distribution of heat at earth's surface. Although not excessively high, some do rear up into the troposphere high enough, for example, to keep cold moist air, coming from Canada, from penetrating California. As another example, mountains may also prevent moisture-bearing winds from delivering their water vapor to such areas as Arizona and New Mexico. Since mountains remain in one place, knowledge of their locations and their effects simplify, rather than complicate, your forecasting. Remember their existence and location, if any are close enough to you to affect your weather.

Energy is required, too, to furnish the heat needed in the process of evaporation. In this, molecules of water are energized to dance harder and faster. Some, near the surface of the water, bounce or are bounced out of it. The surface, incidentally, may be not only the flat surface of an ocean but also the globular-shaped surface of a water droplet. The warmer the water, the faster and harder the molecules dance, and the more rapidly they escape from the water's surface. This is the change from water to vapor.

Evaporation also takes place when clouds dissipate; the energy from the sun furnishes the heat needed in the process. The heat is held by the vapor. This does not raise the vapor's temperature; it is kept in what is called a "latent" form. Later, when this water vapor is condensed, and so changes — not reverses, but changes — from its gaseous form to liquid water, this latent heat is released during the process. Here you see one of the most important sources of heat energy used for work in the processes of the atmosphere. Remember, when water evaporates, heat is absorbed; when water condenses, heat is released.

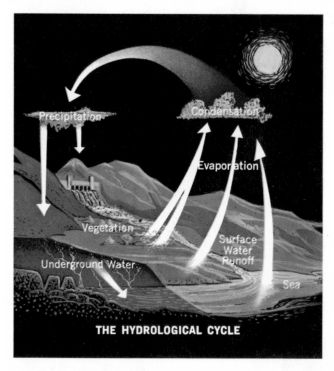

THE HYDROLOGICAL CYCLE

HOW CLOUDS ARE FORMED

When a cloud is formed, the process requires transforming some of the atmosphere's water vapor into a liquid state, as for the cumulus; or into the solid state, as for the ice-crystal cirrus. Condensation accomplishes the first. The second may be accomplished by an action called sublimation. This transformation is direct from gas, a vapor, to solid, or ice — *directly*. (An illustration of the opposite of this process is the eventual disappearance of a camphor ball you had earlier put in a mothproof clothes bag.)

The water droplets or the tiny ice crystals which compose the cloud use a nucleus on which to form. These are present in the atmosphere. Some are sub-microscopic dust particles from soil, volcano, bacteria, smoke particles, or the salt particles that do not fall back into the sea when wave tops are wind-ruffed. There needs to be all, or almost all of the water vapor which can be held in that parcel of air. Then, when that air is cooled sufficiently, clouds form.

The most common method of such cooling takes place when air is lifted because of having been heated or having been pushed up by an uphill draft. As the air rises, the pressure at the higher altitudes is less. Less pressure upon the air permits it to expand. Although the air now has more room, it hasn't acquired any additional molecules. As a result, they don't strike against each other as often, their activity is slowed — and the heat their reduced activity produces is less. Cooling results until the saturation point is reached, and the invisible vapor condenses into visible droplets to begin the cloud. When there are so many droplets that they merge with others, they form drops of rain. Now too heavy to remain supported by air, they fall. If they fall through a cold layer, they may freeze into sleet.

The ground at night cools more than air does. If there is enough moisture in the air just above the ground, and if it is cooled sufficiently, dew forms — not falls, but forms — on the ground where the droplets have touched on it. Then, if the temperature is low enough, and if the sky is clear, there is frost in place of dew.

Updrafts of heated air usually produce, first, the fractocumulus cloud form (cumulus, broken, higher than it is long). If enough heat and moisture continue to be available, fractocumulus develops into fine-weather cumulus. As the day — and its heat — continue to grow, the cloud's base rises. Rising also is the temperature of the air and, therefore, its expansion — *and*, therefore, its condensation level. The cloud grows smaller while it rises, although keeping its cumulus form. Late in the day, when the earth gives to the atmosphere above it more heat than it now is receiving, the cloud lowers. It sinks to levels that are lower and therefore of greater pressure. This results in heating — and visible droplets return once more to invisible vapor. The cloud disappears.

If the thermal lifting is *very* great and so rises to great heights, we say the air is unstable — as compared with the more level layers of less disturbed, stable, air. In such unstable air — and if it also contains enough water vapor — our fair-weather cumulus can be "boiled up" higher into becoming a cumulonimbus. The latent energy which had been stored in the vapor is released in this process of accumulating so large a cloud. Within this towering storm cloud there are turbulence, squalls, thunderstorms, hail, or rain. The violent currents and turbulence of air within the cloud tear apart the water droplets, according to one well-accepted theory, and negative charges of electricity are carried high within the cloud; the protons, low. When these negative and positive charges build high enough, the spark (lightning) jumps the gap, flashing from cloud to cloud or from cloud to ground. Thunder follows: the air, heated by the lightning, expands, cools rapidly, and contracts,

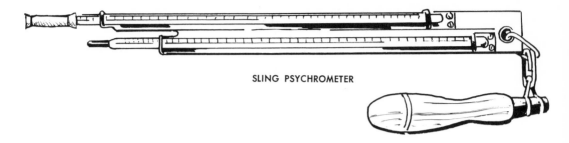

SLING PSYCHROMETER

quickly producing the clap that echoes in rumblings.

Precipitation almost always comes from this cumulonimbus form of cloud. Some types of clouds, however, never yield precipitation; others yield it only occasionally. The very high clouds — cirrus and cirrostratus — are made of ice crystals, so they can never be rainclouds.

Altostratus, at a lower level, may be a rain or snow cloud *if* it is one of the thicker ones. When it is, it produces rain or snow in fairly large quantities. When layers of altostratus are mixed with altocumulus, rain usually follows. When altostratus thickens downward and becomes nimbostratus, expect more intense precipitation with large-size raindrops.

Stratus is wet, too, but in a drizzly or light-snow way; there just isn't enough thickness to this cloud. Stratocumulus does little better; with its slight turbulence, it produces very light rain or snow.

Cumulus or stratus that are broken — fractocumulus or fractostratus — yield no precipitation, probably because they are not thick enough. Fair-weather cumulus never produces rain. But when it builds up vertically on its way to becoming cumulonimbus, it may produce showers. From the cumulonimbus itself come heavy showers. If you do not see the cloud but, instead, see only the heavy showers or hail which come from it, you can identify it as cumulonimbus.

The fact that there are different types of clouds tells that there are various combinations of ways by which these are formed. All is not yet known about cloud formation, and additional reading of cloud physics will be rewarding.

WEATHER INSTRUMENTS

The quantity of water vapor in the atmosphere is called the humidity. It is relative to the air's temperature. To say that the *relative humidity* is 80%, is to say that the air — at a given temperature (and pressure) — has four-fifths of the moisture it could hold before becoming saturated. The *dew point* is the designation for the temperature at which invisible vapor becomes visible droplets.

The instrument to measure relative humidity is the psychrometer — really two thermometers mounted together. There is a regular mercury thermometer to measure the air temperature, then there is a wet-bulb thermometer. The bulb of this second thermometer is covered with a wet moisture-retaining cloth when a reading is wanted. After that, the psychrometer is thoroughly aired; one way is by placing it in front of an electric fan. The wet-bulb thermometer is read again and again until the steadily lowering readings appear to go no lower. These readings go lower because of the cooling which evaporation produces. When a constant air temperature also shows on the other thermometer of the psychrometer, the readings of the two thermometers are recorded. Subtracting the lower wet-bulb reading from that of the dry-bulb thermometer gives the "wet-bulb depression." The meteorologist applies this information to tables prepared by the Weather Bureau and thus determines the air's relative humidity.

Another humidity measuring device is the hair hygrometer. A strand of human hair, attached to a pointer, lengthens or shrinks as moisture in the air increases or decreases. The pointer moves correspondingly over a graded scale. It takes longer for the hair to respond and report than does the wet-bulb thermometer. The hair hygrometer is therefore the less accurate of the two, but it may suffice for your purposes — at least early in your hobby of weather forecasting. If you choose to make your own, you can; this is a simple instrument.

Still generally popular, although perhaps not as accurate as the hair hygrometer, is the little "weather house" with its doll figures, usually of the witch who comes out of the house when the weather will worsen, or the children, when it will turn fair. Instead of a strand of hair, it is a strand of cat-gut which twists when the air's moisture content changes — and so operates the device.

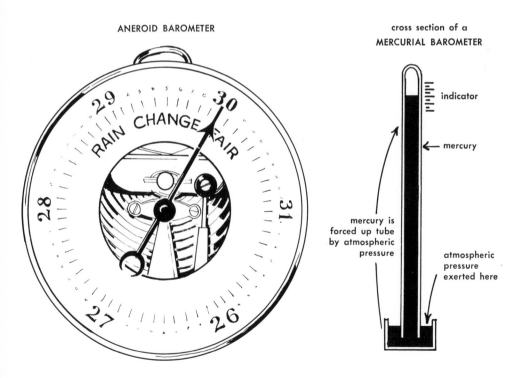

ANEROID BAROMETER

cross section of a
MERCURIAL BAROMETER

indicator

mercury

mercury is
forced up tube
by atmospheric
pressure

atmospheric
pressure
exerted here

You may wish to buy a barometer. Certainly it is desirable for weather forecasting if you go beyond forecasting by clouds and proverbs. The less expensive barometer is the aneroid (unless you are considering the old sailing ship's weatherglass in whose spout the liquid rises when a storm approaches). The aneroid registers barometric pressure by pointer and dial. A moment's reflection will remind you that it is not the present reading but rather the trend of a series of readings by which you will tell what the weather is going to be.

The more expensive and more accurate barometer is the mercurial barometer whose column of mercury rising or falling in its glass tube makes it resemble a thermometer.

If your barometer reads in inches and hundredths, and you wish to convert these into millibars, which are the units of measurement the Weather Bureau and other professionals use, figure 33.86395 millibars to the inch.

A thermometer is a basic requirement and therefore should be as reliable an instrument as you can afford to buy. It should be mounted where the sun's rays won't hit it. If they do, they heat the glass and mercury more than the air, giving an incorrect reading. If you are building your own weather station, the thermometer properly belongs in the instrument shelter. This is an outdoor open-slatted compartment — letting in air but keeping out sun — some two or three feet square, usually standing on legs and the door-opening facing north.

The direction *from* which the wind is blowing is the identification of that wind: a north wind blows from the north. Direction of surface winds is easily identified through movement of leaves, dust, or weather vane. But surface wind direction may differ from the direction of the winds bringing clouds to the same area. *That* direction information comes via nephoscope. This is a horizontal overhead pointer or grid which you align with the direction of the movement of the clouds you are watching — which is then shown by the instrument's pointer against a direction scale. This instrument, too, is easy to build. It is especially useful when you wish to ascertain the directions in which several layers of clouds are moving. Another kind of nephoscope, employing a black-backed mirror, also is easy to build and use. With this you can estimate cloud speed more accurately, although you first need to estimate the cloud's height.

An anemometer measures wind speed at the surface. Although this professional instrument can be duplicated by the amateur, you may be satisfied initially to estimate wind speed by the information of the auxiliary Beaufort Scale.

Visibility usually is part of the weather report. It is the distance, given in miles, which you can see toward the horizon. The amount of precipitation, moisture, or particles in the air will affect visibility. Visibility, then, becomes another tool for you in your forecasting. (A blue-tinted haze indicates clearing. Magnified visibility to the horizon indicates a considerable quantity of moisture — with precipitation likely soon.)

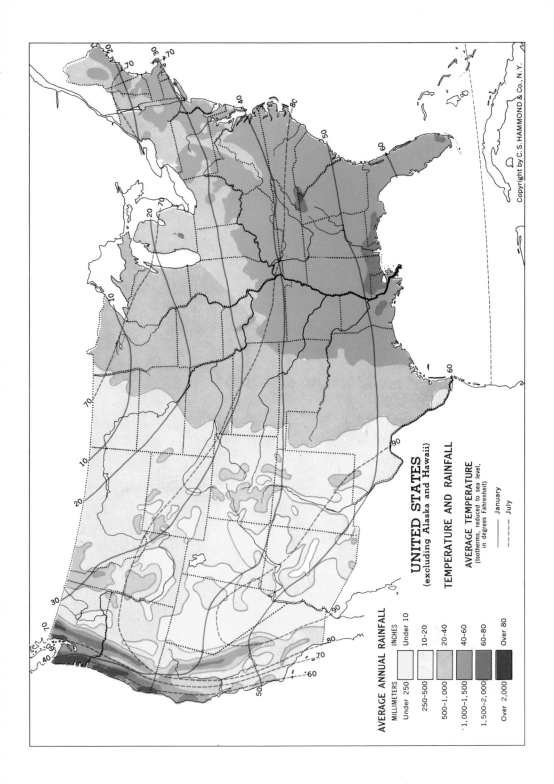

UNITED STATES
(excluding Alaska and Hawaii)

TEMPERATURE AND RAINFALL

AVERAGE TEMPERATURE
(Isotherms, reduced to sea level,
in degrees Fahrenheit)
——— January
- - - - July

AVERAGE ANNUAL RAINFALL

MILLIMETERS	INCHES
Under 250	Under 10
250-500	10-20
500-1,000	20-40
1,000-1,500	40-60
1,500-2,000	60-80
Over 2,000	Over 80

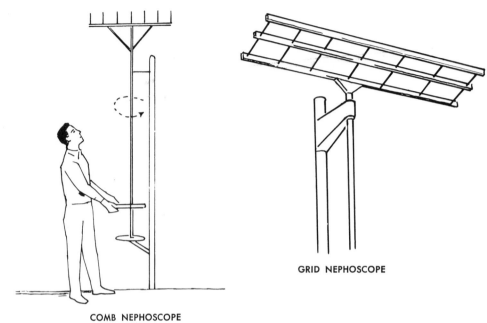

COMB NEPHOSCOPE

GRID NEPHOSCOPE

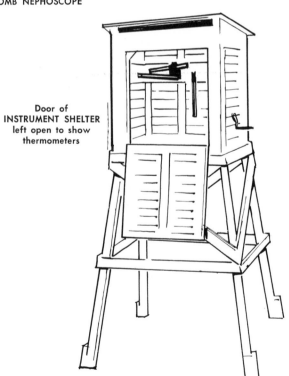

Door of
INSTRUMENT SHELTER
left open to show
thermometers

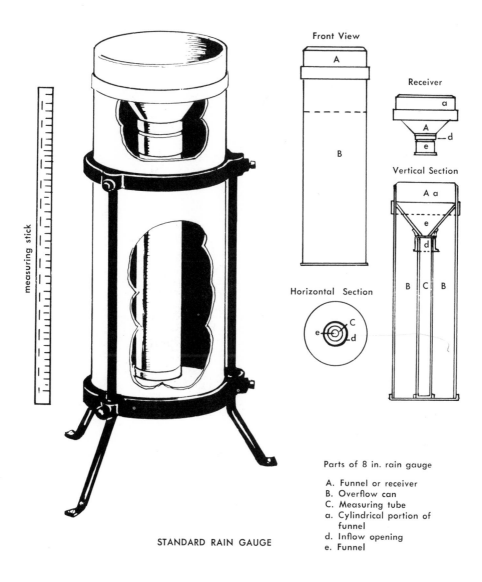

Front View

A

B

Receiver

a

A

d

e

Vertical Section

A a

e

d

B C B

Horizontal Section

C

e

d

measuring stick

STANDARD RAIN GAUGE

Parts of 8 in. rain gauge

A. Funnel or receiver
B. Overflow can
C. Measuring tube
a. Cylindrical portion of funnel
d. Inflow opening
e. Funnel

A rain gauge measures the amount of precipitation during a limited period of time. You may want one in your home weather station so that your records can be complete. This instrument is a container with straight sides open at the top. The quantity of rain found in the container immediately after precipitation is measured in hundredths of an inch. This is difficult to do accurately, therefore most gauges are designed to magnify the depth of rainfall. This gauge consists of a receiver or funnel, a measuring tube, a measuring stick and an overflow can. Many persons construct the measuring tube so that its diameter is one-tenth that of the funnel. One-tenth of an inch of rain will measure, in such a gauge, one inch. (The funnel and tube are not used in measuring snow.)

WEATHER AND OBSERVATION
Equipped with optical systems which can photograph large or small sections of the earth's surface. The image is analyzed electronically, recorded magnetically and, upon command, is telemetered to an earth recording station for interpretation.

Sky cover — the degree to which clouds cover the sky — can be estimated in eighths or in tenths of the sky. The former might be easier for you. Divide the sky in half, then in half again, and then again in half — giving you eight divisions. These are the corresponding designations: first, "clear" if there are no clouds or if they cover less one-eighth of the sky; "scattered" if one-eighth to one-half is cloud-covered; "broken" if one-half to seven-eighths; and "overcast" if more than seven-eighths. Cloud height is difficult to judge without benefit of instruments such as a clinometer. However, practice will assist you in estimating, if you agree that a cloud-height finder is not essential to your hobby.

Your weather observations, made at least twice each day (early and late) at regular times, should include the following — cloud information; types, estimated height, direction, speed, and amount of sky cover; visibility; weather: rain, snow, etc.; temperature; relative humidity and dew point; wind: direction, velocity; barometric pressure; rain (or snow): amount since the last observation; temperatures: maximum and minimum since last observation (requires a special maximum-minimum thermometer or an automatic, constant temperature-recording device — the thermograph); and any remarks concerning the weather which might prove significant. Don't forget to note the date and time of observation.

Although you may make observations such as these only twice daily, certainly you will be watching the weather whenever you look up at the sky.

LOCAL INFLUENCES ON WEATHER

In your observing and forecasting, don't forget the effects of local terrain. Mountains play an important part in the weather of their area. Large bodies of water tend to moderate the temperatures in their area. Mountains and large bodies of water also create local wind effects. These may override the larger pattern of the pressure and wind systems of which your area is one part — and thus affect *your* weather. During the day, land masses grow warmer than do large bodies of water nearby. Air above each also is warmed — more, over the land. That warmer air rises. The less warm air over the nearby sea moves in as a replacement. During the day, then, there is a sea breeze. Air over a mountain slope grows warmer than does air at the same height but farther away from the mountain. The warmer air rises off the mountain slopes and is replaced by air coming in under it. During the day, then, there is a valley breeze.

At night, this condition reverses. The land cools more than the water. Now the cooler air moves from the cooler land to the warmer sea, as a land breeze. Cooler air slides *down* the mountain slopes into the valley, a mountain breeze. In your observations and recordings, it is desirable to distinguish between such local factors and those which have their origin much farther away. Another local factor which could mislead you is the diurnal wind. These are the daily winds which, during the day, normally are quietest at dawn, highest in the midafternoon.

Frequently, a hill sticking up into the airstream will cause a cloud to form — an orographic cloud. This is done by the airstream rising due to flowing *up* the hill. As the air rises, it expands, cools, and forms the cloud. If the hill is high enough, the wind strong enough, the vapor sufficient, the resulting orographic cloud may thicken into a towering cumulus or cumulonimbus. Then comes the rain to the windward side of the high hill. Loss of water from the cloud causes its base to rise, so that it is higher when it has traveled to the lee side of the hill. The air continues to flow *down* the lee side of the hill. As it does, it contracts, heats, and loses its moisture. It reaches the bottom as warm, dry air. This explains why on one side of a hill there may be a chill rain, while on the other side it may be warm and dry.

35

Wendell Kilner

The forecast room of the Weather Bureau office, New York City. The forecaster is plotting movement of weather systems in preparation for formulating the forecast.

THE WEATHER MAP

Many newspapers carry a daily weather map, usually prepared by the U.S. Weather Bureau. From it, and with your knowledge of what makes weather — modified by what you know of weather-influencing factors in your area as revealed by your records — you can attempt weather forecasting on a still more scientific basis. The weather maps of the United States (excepting Alaska and Hawaii) have symbols showing the overall weather of the country as recently as twelve hours ago.

The basis for this information is the reports of observations from Weather Bureau stations in principal cities throughout those 48 states. These cities are shown on the map. A figure alongside indicates the current temperature (F.). Beneath it may be a decimal number indicating precipitation, in inches, that has fallen during the six hours previously. Areas of that precipitation are shaded. Also shown at each station are wind direction, velocity, and sky cover. (Wind speed may be shown per knot: 1.15 mph. 1 mph = 0.87 knots.)

Solid black, curving lines cover the map. These are isobars and connect points reporting the same barometric pressure. Lines which more or less parallel each other form a pressure pattern. Inasmuch as each line is labeled with its pressure (in inches and in millibars), you can identify the pattern as one of a "high" or a "low," depending upon whether the center of the pattern has the highest or the lowest reading within that pattern. You can judge from these highs and lows in which direction the weather may move — in your own area as well as elsewhere throughout the country. Usually this movement is eastward and at a rate of some 700 miles per day in winter, 500 miles in summer. You probably will see a correlation between intensity of wind and closeness of isobars. As you compare the weather maps for a series

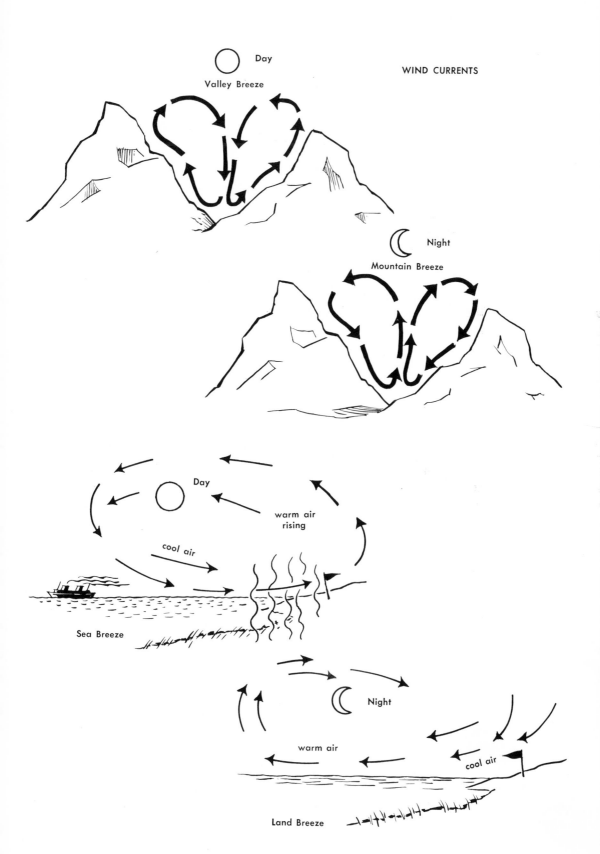

Day

Valley Breeze

WIND CURRENTS

Night

Mountain Breeze

Day

warm air
rising

cool air

Sea Breeze

Night

warm air

cool air

Land Breeze

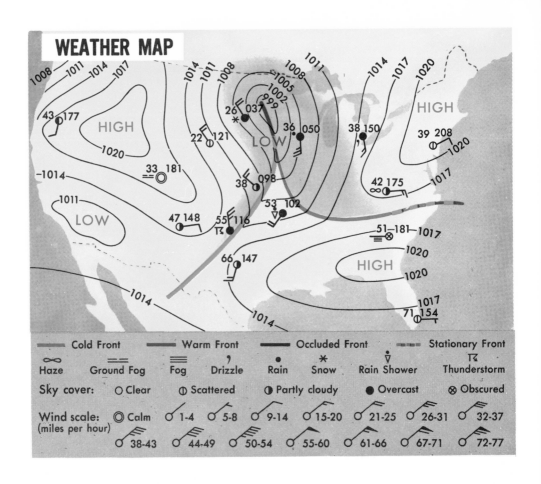

WEATHER MAP

Cold Front ——— Warm Front ——— Occluded Front ——— Stationary Front - - -

Haze ∞   Ground Fog ═   Fog ≡   Drizzle '   Rain •   Snow *   Rain Shower ▽   Thunderstorm

Sky cover: ○ Clear   ① Scattered   ◑ Partly cloudy   ● Overcast   ⊗ Obscured

Wind scale: ◎ Calm   1-4   5-8   9-14   15-20   21-25   26-31   32-37
(miles per hour)   38-43   44-49   50-54   55-60   61-66   67-71   72-77

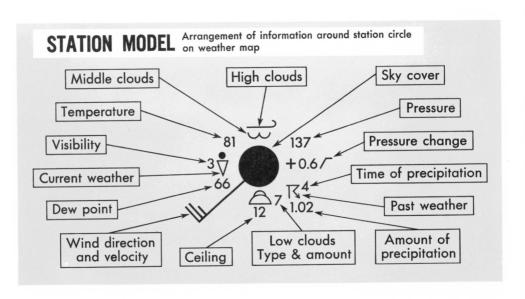

STATION MODEL   Arrangement of information around station circle on weather map

Middle clouds
High clouds
Sky cover
Temperature
Pressure
Visibility
Pressure change
Current weather
Time of precipitation
Dew point
Past weather
Wind direction and velocity
Ceiling
Low clouds Type & amount
Amount of precipitation

81   137   +0.6   3   66   4   7   1.02   12

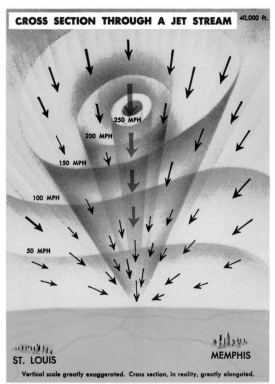

CROSS SECTION THROUGH A JET STREAM 40,000 ft.

250 MPH
200 MPH
150 MPH
100 MPH
50 MPH

ST. LOUIS

MEMPHIS

Vertical scale greatly exaggerated. Cross section, in reality, greatly elongated.

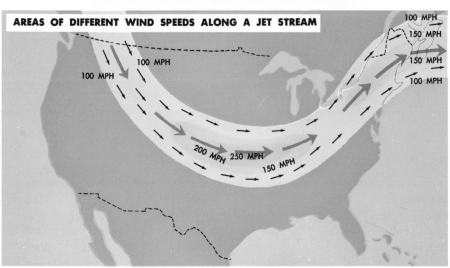

AREAS OF DIFFERENT WIND SPEEDS ALONG A JET STREAM

100 MPH
150 MPH
150 MPH
100 MPH
100 MPH
100 MPH
200 MPH 250 MPH
150 MPH

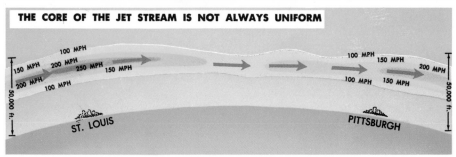

THE CORE OF THE JET STREAM IS NOT ALWAYS UNIFORM

150 MPH
100 MPH
200 MPH
250 MPH 150 MPH
200 MPH
100 MPH

100 MPH 150 MPH
200 MPH
100 MPH 150 MPH

50,000 ft.

ST. LOUIS

PITTSBURGH

50,000 ft.

39

of days, you will see these patterns change in size, shape, location, speed of travel, and intensity. All — including the rate of each change — affect your consideration for forecast.

Winds are associated with these pressure systems, too. The high pressure system consists of heavier (cooler) air, which descends, and flows *outward* from its system's center. Because of earth's rotation, these high-pressure system winds — in the northern hemisphere — are clockwise in their direction. Winds associated with the low-pressure system move in the opposite direction *toward* the center of the system — feeding the rise of air — and revolving counterclockwise around the system's center. Professor Buys-Ballot of the University of Utrecht expressed it simply: if (in the northern hemisphere) you stand with your back to the wind, the pressure is lower on your left hand.

(Navigators of long-range aircraft frequently make use of the winds in high- or low-pressure cells. They chart their course so that the airplane enters into the cell and rides a *tail* wind. This makes for a curving flight part way around the cell. When the airplane reaches the other side of the cell, it leaves and resumes the course it was on before entering the cell. If the area of the Rockies, for example, is dominated by a large cell of high pressure, eastbound flights for New York go via Salt Lake City and Denver — north — to Chicago and then New York. If a low-pressure cell predominates, the flights go via the southern air routes to Chicago and then on to New York. Such riding a tail wind may be the "long way around," but the tail wind makes it the "shortest — in *time* — way home."

This same principle of knowing and traveling *with* weather conditions is followed by the Navy. Like the Air Force, the Navy must pay close attention to the weather. Ships are routed *around* areas of expected bad weather (predicted by the Navy's weather facility). That course may be longer in distance than the original one, but it is shorter in time — and at less cost in ship damage and fuel consumption.)

FRONTS AND YOUR FORECASTS

The surface forming a boundary between two systems which are different from each other is called a "front," after the World War I term for the line of battle between two opposing forces. On the newspaper weather map, this surface boundary is shown as a heavy line. Wording or symbols will reveal which of four kinds of front this one is: a cold front, a warm front, a stationary front, or an occluded front. A cold front is the boundary surface between cold air and a mass of warmer air. The colder, heavier air pushes like a wedge under the warm, lighter air. Usually this kind of front advances southward and eastward.

A warm front is a boundary between warm air and a mass of cooler air. The warm air advances, usually northward and eastward, over a retreating wedge of cooler air.

A stationary front is, as its name suggests, an air mass boundary showing little or no movement. The weather you will find here is the kind usually associated with warm fronts.

An occluded front occurs when two opposing wedges of cold air come together and thereby lift warm air from the earth's surface — frequently resulting in precipitation. (Eventually these three air masses become one.)

You can see, via the symbols on the weather map, how different are the weather conditions on either side of a front: the discontinuities of temperature, cloud cover, wind direction and velocity, precipitation, etc. When a cold or warm front moves over *your* area, you can identify it and determine how far along it has passed over you, by these indications:

COLD FRONT

One has just reached you when earlier cirrostratus, altostratus, or altocumulus changed to cumulonimbus. The front has moved on when the cumulonimbus has broken to fractocumulus and raised to altocumulus with final clearing.

One has just reached you when earlier heavy but short showers changed to squalls or possibly thundershowers. The front has moved on when there is rapid clearing.

One has just reached you when earlier falling of the barometer has reversed to a slight rise. The front has moved on when the barometer shows a sudden rise.

One has just reached you when earlier moderately constant humidity has increased to near-saturation point. The front has moved on when the amount of humidity has dropped rapidly.

One has just reached you when earlier rising temperatures suddenly reverse. The front has moved on when the temperature drops sharply.

One has just reached you when earlier below-normal visibility changed to "poor." The front has moved on when the visibility is very good.

(Winds are generally unchanged during this front's passage. Mostly they are from the S or SW. Before the front arrives, winds also may come out of the W; after it moves on, winds also may come out of the NW.)

WARM FRONT

One has just reached you when earlier cirrus, becoming cirrostratus, changed to nimbostratus. The front has moved on when the nimbostratus has broken to fractostratus and is then followed either by cumulus or clearing.

One has just reached you when earlier steady rain or snow has settled down to persistent rains. The front has moved on when these break into scattered showers or clearing.

One has just reached you when earlier falling of the barometer began to steady. The front has moved on when the barometer holds steady.

One has just reached you when earlier constant, then increasing humidity has reached near-saturation point. This front has moved on when the humidity has reduced to a steady high value.

One has just reached you when former steady temperatures increase gradually and then move rapidly. The front has moved on when the temperature holds steady at a reading higher than it was before the front arrived.

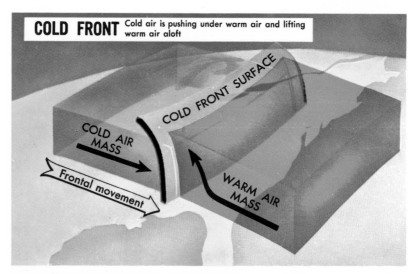

COLD FRONT Cold air is pushing under warm air and lifting warm air aloft

COLD FRONT SURFACE

COLD AIR MASS

Frontal movement

WARM AIR MASS

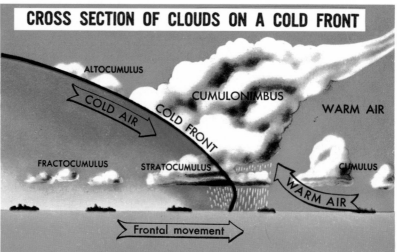

CROSS SECTION OF CLOUDS ON A COLD FRONT

ALTOCUMULUS

CUMULONIMBUS

COLD AIR

COLD FRONT

WARM AIR

FRACTOCUMULUS

STRATOCUMULUS

CUMULUS

WARM AIR

Frontal movement

One has just reached you when earlier fair visibility changed to "poor." The front has moved on when the visibility steadies at below-normal.

(Winds are generally unchanged during this front's passage. Mostly they are from the S or SE; but after the front has arrived or moved on, winds also may be out of the SW.)

Since a cold front moves closer to the ground than does a warm front, friction drags on it, slowing its advance and making its forward surface comparatively steep. This in turn causes accompanying clouds, which can produce heavy precipitation, to develop vertically. In fact, all along the leading edge, bursts of rain are so common that this line is known as the squall line. Clearing and lower temperatures finally follow long after the cold front's passage. Before then, however — only a few hours after the leading edge of the front has passed over — there may be scattered showers. If so, they probably resulted from the cold air mass having moved over ground which was warmer, and more moist. This produces a condition of instability. Showers could then be expected to result.

Remember: as a forecaster, you are concerned with what the weather is going to be. You will, then, use your weather map, your knowledge, and your local observations' record to figure out where the fronts with their highs and lows, their rain or snow or fair weather will be in six or twelve or perhaps twenty-four hours hence. Remember that rain often accompanies lows; but that there must be a supply of moist air, too, available from a direction which is consistent with the direction of the low's movement. Just how the front behaves will depend, in good part, on the difference in humidity and temperature between the two systems.

In a warm front, the warm air flows gradually up a slope of cold air which may reach a height of five miles and be hundreds of miles long. This ascension lowers the temperature of the warm air which, in addition, is moist.

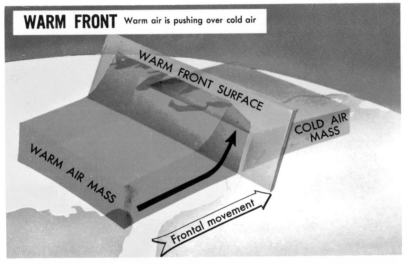

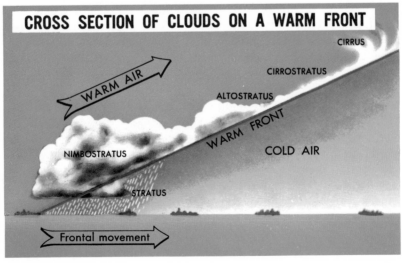

Drizzly stratus clouds result and become rain as these clouds build to nimbo-stratus with the continuing rise of the warm air over the colder air. The rising continues with the forming of higher-level clouds such as altostratus and then cirrostratus, until the warm air has at last surmounted the highest of the cold air mass. Here cirrus forms — the mare's tails whose appearance signals to the observer on the ground that an approaching warm front along the ground is some five hundred miles and about one day away. As the front nears, these high clouds give way to the lower, heavier, darker ones until, finally, precipitation occurs.

Air masses such as these are quite large, yet are characterized by having virtually similar temperatures and humidities throughout. They acquired these temperature and humidity characteristics from the region over which they were formed and from which they were torn loose and moved away by the large air currents resulting from earth's spinning. As they traveled over other areas, they may also have acquired the characteristics of these, depending, in part, upon how slowly they passed over them.

Such originating regions are called source regions. The mass of air (sometimes a thousand miles across) must remain over the source region long enough to acquire its characteristics. That requires the stability which only a high-pressure — not a low-pressure — area can provide. The source regions for the air masses which affect our weather in the continental United States are the following: Alaska and Canada for cold dry air masses; the polar portions of the Atlantic and Pacific Oceans for cold moist air masses; the tropical portions of the Atlantic Ocean and Gulf of Mexico for warm moist air masses; and the northern portion of Mexico for warm dry air masses. These source regions are identified as Polar Canadian, Polar Pacific, and Polar Atlantic; and Tropical Gulf, Atlantic, and Tropical Continental.

THE LARGER PICTURE INCLUDES THE HELP OF COMPUTERS

Over all is the general circulation of our earth's atmosphere — the curving movements of air surrounding this spinning rock hurtling through space. A description of this circulation starts with the rising of heated air — this time at the belt around earth's girth, the equator, upon which the sun's rays fall most directly and therefore heat most. The air rises and then begins to cool. It descends and drifts toward the cold-air poles in a curved line, because of earth's spinning; our atmosphere is held only loosely to earth's surface. Earth's rotation also breaks it into currents of different directions. In our northern hemisphere, the Trade Winds are in the area from the equator north to about 30° N. These blow generally from NE to SW. At this 30° N latitude, there is a break between these Trades and the Prevailing Westerlies which blow from SW to NE from 30° N to 60° N. The dividing line between these two wind systems is the Subtropical High — a high pressure area which breeds almost-permanent great islands of clear, dry air called subtropical anticyclones. These contribute considerably to the generally fine weather of our continental United States. North of 60° N are the Polar

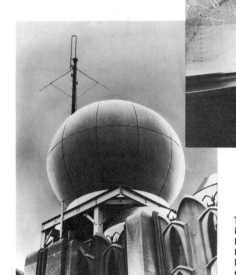

Radar meteorologist plotting precipitation echoes on the radarscope. Map on the wall shows previously reported echoes and their movement.

The radar dome atop the R.C.A. building in New York City is used by the Weather Bureau to detect weather conditions. Pulses sent out by radar are reflected back and shown visually on a cathode-ray tube.

courtesy U.S. Weather Bureau

Easterlies. This cold air tends to move south from the Pole and is deflected westward by earth's rotation. Since it cannot flow uninterrupted to the equator, it is imprisoned within its area — until so much accumulates that it breaks out and occasionally invades us with its bitter-cold weather.

In the future, worldwide weather information will be collected and fed into computers for greater accuracy in weather forecasting. This information will be sought by weather satellites and specially instrumented rockets and balloons, by radar and electronic computers, and by meterologists in isolated weather stations and on ice sheets floating in the Arctic seas or at the bottom of the world in the frozen Antarctic — and right here. Countries join together, even those which have differences in other matters, to learn how to improve their knowledge of the causes of weather and how to predict it more accurately — eventually, perhaps, doing something about it. Artificial rainmaking has its supporters as well as its doubters. But the problem of eventual water shortage may be made fertile. Inhospitable climates may be softened. Still more accurate, prompt, and distant weather information must be provided as air travel increases in altitude, speed, and amount.

Weather forecasting is an increasingly important activity. Its requirements for scientifically correct information continually increase. The amateur who has observed accurately and has kept accurate records may even be able to make a contribution of information which might fill the one remaining gap in an otherwise complete piece of information.

Certainly, the more knowledge which the forecaster — professional *or* amateur — acquires, and the better he uses it, the more accurate will be his answer to that age-old, deceptively simple question:

"What will the weather be?"

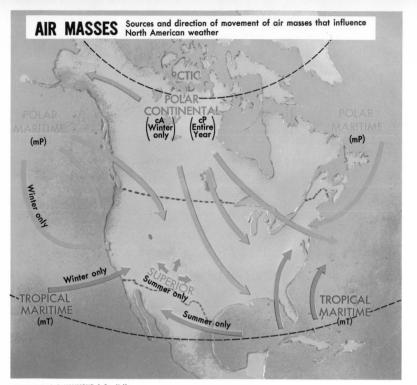

AIR MASSES Sources and direction of movement of air masses that influence North American weather

ARCTIC AND POLAR CONTINENTAL

cA (Winter only) cP (Entire Year)

POLAR MARITIME (mP)

POLAR MARITIME (mP)

Winter only

Winter only

SUPERIOR Summer only

Summer only

TROPICAL MARITIME (mT)

TROPICAL MARITIME (mT)

RAIN

▽ Light or moderate

▽ Heavy

== Ground

↘ Mild

∧ Squally weather

THE SCIENCE-HOBBY SERIES

PRESENT WEATHER

PRECIPITATION

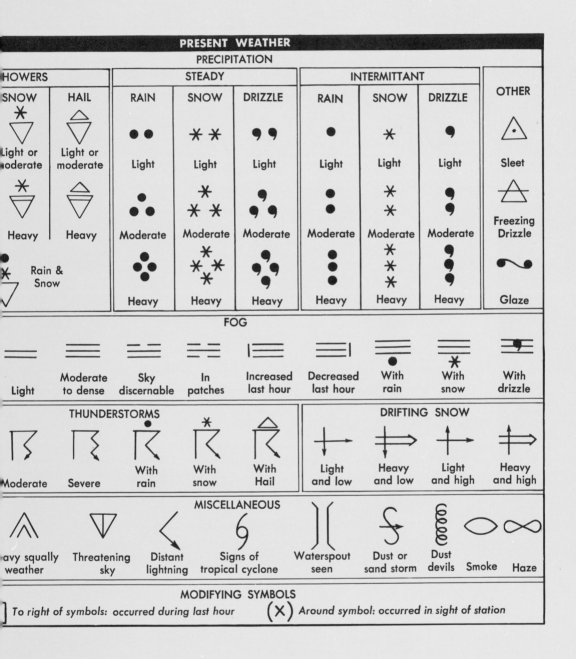

SHOWERS		STEADY			INTERMITTANT			OTHER
SNOW	HAIL	RAIN	SNOW	DRIZZLE	RAIN	SNOW	DRIZZLE	
Light or moderate	Light or moderate	Light	Light	Light	Light	Light	Light	Sleet
Heavy	Heavy	Moderate	Moderate	Moderate	Moderate	Moderate	Moderate	Freezing Drizzle
Rain & Snow		Heavy	Heavy	Heavy	Heavy	Heavy	Heavy	Glaze

FOG

| Light | Moderate to dense | Sky discernable | In patches | Increased last hour | Decreased last hour | With rain | With snow | With drizzle |

THUNDERSTORMS

| Moderate | Severe | With rain | With snow | With Hail |

DRIFTING SNOW

| Light and low | Heavy and low | Light and high | Heavy and high |

MISCELLANEOUS

| Heavy squally weather | Threatening sky | Distant lightning | Signs of tropical cyclone | Waterspout seen | Dust or sand storm | Dust devils | Smoke | Haze |

MODIFYING SYMBOLS

To right of symbols: occurred during last hour   (X) Around symbol: occurred in sight of station

47

We specialize in publishing quality books for
young people. For a complete list please write

LERNER PUBLICATIONS COMPANY

241 First Avenue North, Minneapolis, Minnesota 55401